Early Childhood Scientific Brain Connections

Early Childhood Scientific Brain Connections

Clementine T. Fordham

To order additional copies of this book, contact:
Xlibris Corporation
1-888-795-4274
www.Xlibris.com
Orders@Xlibris.com
66692

Extending and Preparing Early Childhood Students for Future Scientific Success

An early childhood developmentally appropriate scientific guide for students to comprehend factual scientific information and involve in first-hand experiences in order to exceed and will direct them into present and future science success with staff, parents and volunteer's dedicated assistance.

Clementine Fordham

Many thanks to:

Jackie McNeil
Ilene West
Linda Ferdinand
For your cooperation!

Illustrators:

Jesse Knowlin
James Price

This Manual is dedicated to my loving children

Kathy, James & Sabrina

Also to my caring nieces

Vickie & Sharon

And to all of my grandchildren and great grandchildren.

I thank God for my family.

PREFACE

No matter what areas of science you are planning to include in your curriculum; this manual is presented to extend, explore, experience and create appropriate developmental skills that will cause early childhood students to understand why, when and what takes place in their environment as pre-school children.

The manual is arranged into scientific subject areas. Each lesson will present: The subject area, the lesson number, the focus point, word pronunciation and meanings, materials needed, first-hand experiences, and the instructional lesson.

Discussions and oral quizzes will be used as a diagnostic practice.

The entire manual focuses on all pre-school children who can participate and be able to experiment with activities learned (with supervision).

Students are inquirers and have lots of fun finding out what is.

Be happy and your students will be happy too! Be a good motivator about scientific things around us.

Learning takes place best when the students are motivated and interested in the lessons you are presenting. Students enjoy discovering science facts for themselves.

This manual will help students develop additional facts, ask questions and discuss their understanding. It is sincerely hoped that students will comprehend each lesson so success will be experienced in future science tests.

My first reason for "Extending and Preparing Early Childhood Students for Future Scientific Success" came about as a sincere desire to assist students at an early level, so by the time they reach third and fifth grade levels, they will succeed with higher scores on the State Comprehension Science Assessment Scores.

It is imperative that there must be early childhood science interventions, in order for our students to acquire scientific knowledge in out scientific world.

The Employment Projections are on the following pages: Which will your child choose?

EMPLOYMENT PROJECTIONS

The fastest growing occupations projected to have the largest numerical increases in employment between 2006-2016 by level of post secondary education or training.

From a scientific point, their are the fastest growing occupations: beginning veterinarian, pharmacists, chiropractors, physicians and surgeons, optometrists, computer information scientists researchers, biochemists and biophysics, clinical counseling, and school psychologists, metal health counselors, mental health and substance abuse physical therapists, physician assistants, network system analysts, computer software engineers, behavioral disorder counselors, veterinarians technologists and technicians, skin care, manicurists and pedicurists, fitness trainers audio and video equipment technicians, meter machines, medical assistants, pharmacy technicians, dental assistants, personal and home care aides, home health aides, electricians, cooks, food preparers, hairdressers, cosmetologists, practical and licensed vocation nurses, nurses aides, dental hygienists, registered nurses, computer system analysts, computer software engineers, rehabilitation counselors, mental health and substance abuse, social workers, medical scientists, child care workers.

With the possibility of students choosing one of the fastest growing occupations is one of my main reasons for wanting to "Extend and Prepare Early Childhood Students for their future scientific success", he/she chooses.

We can and should not put comprehending scientific knowledge on the "back burners".

Extending and Preparing Early Childhood Students for Future Scientific Success

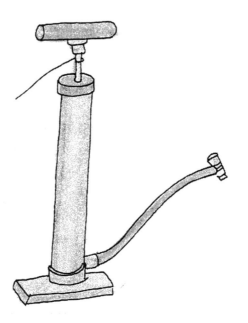

LESSON ONE

Title: Air

Focus: What and where is air?

Vocabulary Development: Atmosphere, surround, odorless, tasteless, colorless, substance, scientist, grind, wind, push, wheat, windmill, pinwheel, earth.

Materials Needed: Straws, tape, construction paper

First-hand equipment: Making a pinwheel and go outdoors to discover the directions of the wind.

Lesson

The atmosphere surrounding the earth is called, air. It is odorless, tasteless, colorless, and does not have a special shape, but large in size. The air is made up of other substances. The wind is a force of moving air. The wind can do work. A strong wind can knock down trees, but it can help us too. A long time ago windmills were used to grind wheat and corn to make flour. The blades of the windmill caught the wind as it turned like a pinwheel.

Christopher Columbus, a scientist put up sails on his sailboat for the force of the wind to push his sailboats across the ocean.

Air

Directions for making a pinwheel:

Instructions: Cut slits in a square piece of construction paper. Do not cut all the way to the center of the square. Fold the four corners to the middle and push a tooth pick through them. **Place a bead?????** Push the tooth pick through a plastic drinking straw, a bead, and piece of cork. Blow on the pinwheel to make it spin.

Vocabulary

Across—front side to side

Air-the atmosphere surrounding the earth.

Atmosphere—layers of gases around the earth.

Caught—to catch

Colorless—without color, dull

Corn—kernels on large ears

Down—in a lower place

Earth—the planet we live on, ground

Flour—powdered substance made by sifting grains

Force—full strength

Grind—to crush

Knock—to make a thumping noise

Large—bigger than others of its kind

Moving—to change the place or position

Odorless—scentless

Ocean—a huge body of water that covers three-fourth of the earth's surface

Pinwheel—a small wheel with colored vanes pinned to a stick so as to revolve in the wind

Push—to press against a thing so as to move it

Sails—a strong fabric used to catch the wind to cause a ship to move

Sailboat—a boat that is propelled by means of a snail or sails

Scientist—a specialist in science knowledge.

Shape—the finish form in which something may appear

Size—a thing which determines how much shape it covers

Special—of or for a particular purpose

Strong—forceful

Substance—the real or essential part of something

Surrounding—to circle all or nearly all sides

Tasteless—to taste the flavor of something by putting it in your mouth

Turned—to move around or partly around

Wheat—used for making flour

Windmill—a mill operated by the winds rotating of large vanes radiating from a shaft

Work—something made or done

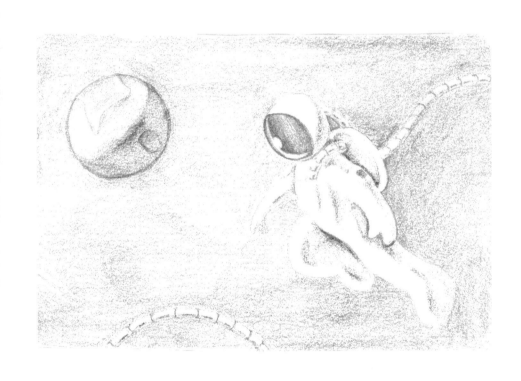

LESSON TWO

Title: Astronauts

Focus: Who are they and what they do?

Vocabulary Development: Astronaut, rockets, space, shutter, mission, NASA (National Aeronautics Space Administration), gravity, opposite, stages, satellites, equipment, airplanes, long, engines, fast, test, life.

Materials Needed: Crayons, construction paper, balloons, table, ball.

First hand experiment: To discover that every movement there is an opposite movement.

Directions:

Blow-up a balloon, tie the open end to keep air from getting out.

Place it on a table.

Watch it: Did it move? If a force is pushing or pulling it, then it will move.

Blow up another balloon, do not tie the end, instead, hold the end very tightly, so no air will get out.

Now, let it go: Did it move?

Throw a ball in the air: What happenend?

There are three stages before a spaceship lifts off:

Stage One: A powerful engine has many rockets, one on top of the other, to get the rocket straight up in the air.

Stage Two: When the engine is fired, it burns out and falls to the earth

Stage Three: The rocket moves very fast around the earth

The first satellite did not send people, but was used to test equipment

In school, astronauts learn about the space shuttle and how to operate it. They must get use to living and working in space. The space shuttle is the only spaceship that takes-off like a rocket and lands like and airplane. When you go into space, it is called a mission. They are going into space to discover answers to many unknown questions about space.

Space has little pull. Everything floats therefore spaceships have to move very, very fast to get out of gravity's pull.

What would you like to do in space?

Would you like to become an astronaut?

Vocabulary

Airplane—a motor drive aircraft kept aloft by the force of air upon its wing

Another—an additional: one more

Answer—a reply

Astronauts—a person trained to make rocket flights in outer space.

Ball—any round object

Balloons—a large airtight bag that rises when filled with a gas lighter than air.

Become—to come of grow to be

Blow—to f air from into, onto or through

Burn—the firing of a rocket engine in space

Discover—to learn of something first

Earth—the planet we live on

End—The last part of anything

Engine—any machine that uses energy to develop mechanical power

Equipment—an equipping or being equipped

Fast—rapidly

Fired—the flame, heat and light of combustion

First—before any other

Floats—anything that stays on the top of liquid

Power

Gravity—The force that pulls things into the center of the earth. It also pulls the planets toward the sun.

Hold—to keep in a certain position or condition

Land—the solid part of the earth's surface

Lift—to bring up to a higher position; raise

Like—Equal; having the same characteristics

Living—a live; having life

Long—Greater than usual length

Mission—A task to be carried out

Movement—A moving or manner of moving

NASA—School for training Astronauts

Open—not closed

Operate—to be in action; work

Opposite—Placed on the opposing side

People—All the persons of a racial of ethnic group

Place—the part of the space occupied by a person or thing

Powerful—Strong; mighty

Pull—to exert force on or to move toward or force

Push—to press against a thing so as to move it

Rocket—a device that moves very fast caused by gaseous combustion

Satellite—a small planet revolving around something that circles planets

School—a place to be educated

Shuttle—has tow parts, one for the Astronaut and the booster rockets and fuel tank. They may be reused.

Space—the area above the earth's atmosphere

Stages—a period in process of development

Straight—No bends

Table—a piece of furniture having a flat top and a set of legs

Takes-off—the act of leaving the ground, as in jumping or flight

Test—questions to determine a person's knowledge gaine

Throw—to send through the air rapidly

Tightly—strong; closely together

Top—the highest part of anything

Very—complete

Working—the act used in work

Would—condition

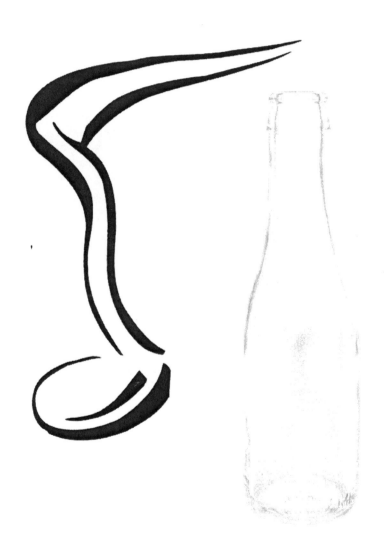

LESSON THREE

Title: Bottle music

Focus: How do we create low and high music sounds?

Vocabulary Development

Create, discover, music, high, low, water, sounds, pitch

Material needed: Bottles (five, same size and shape), water and food coloring.

First hand experiment:

Directions:

Place water in the first bottle almost to the top.

Place the second bottle three fourths full.

Place third bottle half full of water.

Place the fourth bottle a quarter full of water.

Leave the last bottle empty.

Use different food coloring for the first four bottles

Blow across the top of each bottle (preferably individually, if not, please use sanitized tissues to clean off the top of each bottle after use.

When there is very little air in the bottle, there is a higher pitch. When there is more air, the pitch is lower.

Have students sing a known song that begins with one of the pitches.

Discuss the results.

Vocabulary

Across—from one side to the other

Almost—very nearly but not all

Begin—to start doing

Blow—to move with some force

Bottle—a container of liquids, usually made of glass, plastic having a narrow neck

Create—bring into being

Different—not alike

Discover—to be the first to find out

Each—every one of two or more considered separately

Empty—having nothing in it

Full—having in it all there is space for

Fourth—any of the four equal parts of something

High—of more than normal height, extending

Known—pp. of know

Low—not far above the ground

More—greater in amount; additional

Music—the art of combining sounds in melody; rhythmic sequence of pleasing sounds

Pitch—the quality of a tone or sound

Quarter—any of the four equal parts of something

Second—a very short period of time

Sing—to make musical sounds or notes with the voice

Sound—vibrations in air; to express or indicate

Three—the number between two and four

Top—a lid, cover or cap

Use—to bring into action

Water—the colorless liquid occurring on earth as rivers, lakes, oceans, and falling from the clouds as rain.

LESSON FOUR

Title: Clouds

Focus: How are clouds formed?

Vocabulary Development: Formed, cloud, condensation, breathe, mirror, windowpane, trickling, tiny, cue, heat, vapor, against, background, drop, freeze, water, bottle, cold, ice.

Material needed: A mirror, window-pane, a glass bottle, and ice cube, hot (adult handle only) water.

First hand experiment:

    A. Breath on the mirror or windowpane.

    B. Wait a while.

Look at the mirror or window pane

You should see tiny drops of water trickling down the mirror or windowpane

Clouds are made up of many water drops

If clouds move into warmer air, you can't see them anymore, but if it moves into cooler air, the water drops may freeze and fall as snow

Let's see if we can make our own clouds

Directions:

Fill the bottle with hot (adult) water. Let it stand for a few minutes.

Pour most of the water away. Keep about two inches in the bottom of the bottle.

Place the ice cube on top of the bottle.

Place the bottle against a dark background

Watch to see what happens

The hot water will heat the air above it. This air will move up to the cold ice cube. The water vapor in the rising air should form a small cloud.

There are many types of clouds. Rain falls from clouds.
Allow students to talk or describe clouds they saw.

Vocabulary

About—on very side; all round

Above—in a higher place

Against—in opposition to

Anyone—no matter which of more than two

Away—from any given place

Background—surface against which something is seen

Bottle—a container for liquids made of glass or plastic and having a relatively narrow nect.

Bottom—the lowest part of; the under on which something rest

Breathe—to take air into the lungs and let it out again

Cannot—no choice

Clouds a visible mass of condensed water vapor suspended in the atmosphere, consisting of minute droplets or ice crystals.

Cold—of a temperature much lower than that of the human body; chilly.

Condensation—the reduction of a gas to a liquid

Cooler—a container for keeping things cold

Cube—a solid with six equal square sides

Dark—entirely or partly without light

Drop—a very small round of liquid

Fall—to come down by the force of gravity

Formed—the shape or outline of anything; structure apart from color and material

Freeze—to be formed into ice

Glass—a hard brittle substance

Heat—the quality of being hot

Ice—the glassy, brittle, form of water made solid by frozen water

Inches—a measure of length; a very small amount

Keep—to observe or pay reward; to maintain.

Look—to direct one's eyes to see

Make—to shape by putting together

Minutes—the sixteenth part of a unit: 1/60 of an hour

Mirror—a smooth surface that reflects the images of objects

More—greater in amount

Most—greatest in amount

Move—to change the place or position

Own—Belonging to one self

Rain—water falling to the earth in drops that have been condensed from the moisture in the atmosphere.

Rising—that rises, going up. Upward

See—to get knowledge by seeing, observing through the eyes

Should—obligation, duty, propriety

Small—little in size

Snow—particles of water vapor which when in the upper air fall to the earth as soft white flakes.

Stand—to be or remain in a generally upright position supported on its base, bottom.

Them—a linking verb: that's them

Then—at that time

Types—a kind of group with distinguishing characteristics in common

Tiny—very small

Top—the highest part

Trickling—to flow slowly in a thin stream or drops

Two—the cardinal number between one and three

Up—from a lower to higher place

Vapor—visible particles of moisture floating in the air

Wait—to stay in a place; remain

Warmer—having or giving off a degree of heat

Water—the colorless liquid occurring on earth or rivers, lakes, oceans, falling from the clouds as rain.

Window pane—a pane of glass in a window

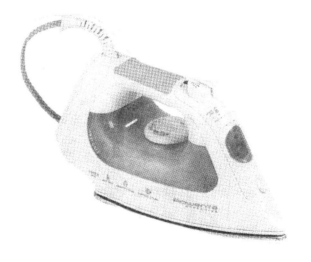

LESSON FIVE

Title: Energy

Focus: What is Energy?

Vocabulary Development: Energy, cause, move, force, thoughts, muscles, clock, farmers, plow, animals, crayons, wagons, waterwheels, something, push, pull, construction paper.

Material Needed: A clock, comb, pencil, crayon, bell, picture, magazines, blocks, box, two small boats, pin, corks, sail paper, and balloons.

If you put forth an effort to move something, this is called, "force." It can be a push or a pull.

First hand experiment:

Directions:

Lift a stack of five blocks

Use your muscles to pull a small block

Ring a bell

Watch the clock

Find pictures in a magazine of items that are working

Anything that can do work, which causes something to move is energy. If nothing moves, it does not work.

Animals were taught to do hard work. Horses learned to pull wagons and plow for the farmers. Waterwheels were a force for running water.

Ask your parents to tell you what items you have at home that causes something to move.

Draw pictures of items that work.

Vocabulary

Animal—Any such organism other than a human being, plant or bacterium.

Anything—A thing no matter of what kind.

Balloon—A large air flight bag that rises and lighter than air that floats above earth when filled with hot air.

Bell—A bellow object usually cuplike made of metal or other hard material, which rings when struck.

Blocks—Any large, solid piece of wood, stone, or metal often with flat surfaces.

Boat—A small open watercraft propelled by oars, sails, or an engine.

Box—Any of various kinds of container usually rectangular.

Can—A container of various kinds usually made of metal with a separate cover.

Card board—Wood or other stiff materials.

Cause—A reason, motive, or ground for some action, feelings.

Corks—The lights, thick, elastic outer bark of an oak tree.

Effort 1—The using of energy to get something done.

Energy—What makes people and machines able to do work. (Fuels, water, wind, etc.)

Farmers 2—A person who earns his living by farming.

Find—Come upon; meet with discover by chance.

Five—The cardinal number between four and six.

Force 2—A physical power or strength exerted against a person or thing.

Forth—Forward in place, time degree; onward.

Hard—Not easily dented.

Horses—Any of several varieties of large, strong animals with four legs, solid hoofs and flawing mane and tail.

Item 1—An article, unit, separate things.

Learned—To get knowledge of a subject or skill.

Lift—To pick up and move: To hold up.

Magazines—A publication usually with a paperback and sometimes illustrated. That or regular intervals, contains stories, articles.

Move—To change the place of position of.

Muscles 1—Any of the body organs consisting of bundles of cells that can be contracted and expanded to produce bodily movement.

Nothing—No thing; not anything

Pictures—An images of an object, person.

Pin—A peg of metal used to fasten or holding things together.

Plow—A farm implemented used to cut, turn up and break-up the soil.

Pull—To exert force to cause to move toward the source of the force; drag, draw

Push—To exert force against

Put—To drive or send by a thrust; to force; to cause something to be in a certain place or position.

Ring—A small circular band of metal\

Running—The act of a person that runs

Small—Little in size; not large.

Stack—Any somewhat orderly pile

Something—A thing that is not definitely known.

Taught 1—of teach

Two—The cardinal number between one and three.

Wagons—Any of various types of four wheeled vehicles pulled or stored

Watch—To look or observe

Waterwheels—A wheel turned by water, running against or on paddles used as a source of power.

LESSON SIX

Title: Fog

Focus: What is Fog?

Vocabulary Development: Fog, difficult, mass, air, temptation, outline, runway, foghorns, kinds, heavy, light, ground, moist, surface, blanket, thick, continue, drifts, wind, indicate, nearness, airplanes, signals, ships.

Information

Lesson

Fog moves over or close to land and water. It is a mass of air with water vapors. The fog makes transportation by ships, airplanes and automobiles experience difficult visually seeing their route.

Fog develops when warm moist air rises over a cold surface i.e. land, ice or water.

There are signals used that will indicate your nearness. Colored lights are used by cars, and by airplanes to indicate the outline of a runway. Ships use foghorns to indicate their location.

There are different kinds of fog: heavy fog, light fog, steam fog, ground fog, up slope fog are some.

Under the tight conditions, the warm air cools and fog forms in a thick blanket that may continue for days, it drifts with the wind.

Allow students to talk about whether they have ever observed a fog.

Vocabulary

Air—Space above the earth, breeze, wind.

Airplane—An aircraft heavier than air, that is kept aloft by the force of air upon it wings and is driven forward by a screw propeller.

Automobile—A passenger car, usually four wheeled, propelled by an engine or motor. Automobiles travel on streets or roads.

Blanket—A large piece of soft wool cloth used for warmth on a bed as cover.

Close—Shut; not open.

Cold—Temperature much lower than that of the human body; very chilly.

Colored—Having color.

Cool—Moderately cold; neither warm nor very cold.

Condition—Anything essential to the existence or occurrence of something; to bring in the proper existence.

Continue—to remain in existence: To go on in a specified course of action or condition.

Days—The period of light between sunrise and sunset.

Develops—To cause to grow gradually in same way.

Difficult—Hard to do or make. Understand.

Drift—An act or instance of being driven or carried along.

Either—One or the other (of two).

Fog—A large mass of vapor condensed to fine particles just above earth's surface.

Foghorn—A horn blown to give warning to ships in the fog.

Ground—the lowest part, base, or bottom of anything; the surface of the earth; the soil of the earth.

Heavy—Hard to lift because of great weight.

Indicate—To direct attention to; to point to or point out.

Kinds—Essential character; sort; variety; class.

Land—the solid part of the earth's surface not covered by water.

Light—brightness. The way in which something is seen, not dark.

Location—Locating or being located; position in space.

Mass—A quantity of matter forming a body of indefinite shape and size, relatively large size; lump.

Moist—Slightly wet; damp.

Nearness—At or to a short distance in space or time.

Outline—A line bounding the limits of an object, showing its shape; cantour line.

Over—A position up from; higher than above.

Rides—person who rides.

Right—Some set standards.

Route—Roadway or course for traveling

Runway—A strip of leveled, usually paved ground, for use by airplanes in taking off and landing.

Ships—Any vessel of considerable size—navigating deep water.

Signals—Indication, a sign or event fixed or understand as the occasion for action.

Steam—Water as converted into an invisible vapor by being; heated to the boiling point.

Surface—The outer face of an object.

Thick—Having great depth; not thin.

Transportation—A transporting or being transported.

Under—A position down from, lower than: below.

Visually—Of connected with, or used in seeing.

Warmer—Having or giving off a moderate degree of heat.

Water Vapor—Water in the form of mist or tiny diffused particles.

Wind—Air in motion.

LESSON SEVEN

Title: Gravity affects how plants grow.

Focus: What is gravity?

Vocabulary Development—gravity, downward, objects, toward, earth, force, plants, grow, cradle, side, upright, upside down, center.

Materials Needed: dried beans, three ten ounce plastic foam cups potting soil, tray, masking tape, string, pencil, and camera.

Lesson and Experiments

If you jump out of a tree (low branch) what keeps you from going up in space? We go down because gravity pulls us downward. It is a force that pulls all objects toward the earth.

Let's see if this is true about plants.

First-hand Experiment:

Directions:

Soak twelve beans in water for twelve hours.

Use a pencil to punch holes in the bottom of the cups.

Fill the cups with potting soil and put them in the tray.

Soak the soil with water then let it drain

Punch four holes one half inch deep into the soil in each cup. (Space the holes at an equal distance from each other, and one half inch from the rim of the cup).

Take out twelve of the soaked beans. (Make sure the beans have no spots, they are unbroken and not cracked).

Plant four beans in each of the holes you punched inside of the cups. Cover them with the soil and water them lightly.

Within five days or until the beans have grown about two inches high, lightly water them again.

Take one of the cups and use masking tape to make a cradle. (Be careful to tape around the young plants without touching them. Your taped cradle should hold the soil in the cup, when you turn it upside down).

Hang this cup upside down away from direct sunlight

Set one of the other cups on its side away from direct sunlight.

The third cup keeps growing upright and away from direct sunlight.

Check your plants at eight, twenty-four and forty-eight hours. Take pictures.

At the end of three days, carefully remove the soil and plants from the cups. Gently shake the soil from the roots of the plants and look and talk about the differences. Take pictures.

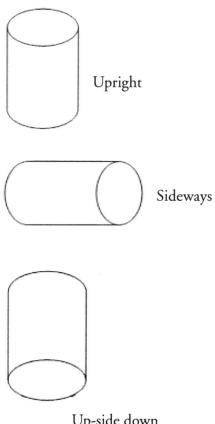

Upright

Sideways

Up-side down

Place masking tape
between plants to hold
soil in.

Plants grow away from the center of the earth toward the sky.

Plants grow away from gravity's pull.

Vocabulary

About—On every side; all around.

Affects—To have an effect on.

Again—Back into a former position.

Because—For the reason or cause that; on account of the fact that, since.

Bottom—The lowest or last place or position; the underside; underneath

Camera—A device for taking photographs.

Carefully—Acting in a thoughtful way; cautious; guarded.

Center—The point around which anything revolves.

Cover—To place something on or over, or in front of, to conceal, protect; or close.

Cradle—A baby's small bed, usually.

Cups—A small open container for beverages; usually bowl shaped and with a handle.

Days—The periods of light between sunrise and sunset.

Differences—Condition, qualify, fact, or instance of being different.

Direct—By the shortest ways, without turning or stopping; not round about, straight.

Drain—To draw off liquid gradually.

Dried beans—Dry beans

Down—From a higher to a lower place toward the ground or in three dimensions, within which all things exists.

Downward—Toward a lower place or position.

Earth—The planet that we live on.

Eight—The cardinal number between seven and nine.

Equal—Of the same quality, size, number, value.

Five—The cardinal number between four and six.

Foam—the whitish mass of bubbles formed in liquid by agitation, fermentation.

Force—Strength; energy power.

Forty eight

Four—The cardinal number between three and five.

Gently—In a gentle manner or degree.

Going—The act of one who goes.

Gravity—The force that pulls things into the center of the earth.

Grow—To come into being or being produced naturally; spring up; sprout.

Hang—To attach to something above with no support from below. Suspend.

High—To take and keep with the hands, arms or other means; grasp.

Holes—A hollowed out place; pit

Hours—A division of time; one of the twenty-four parts of a day; sixty minutes.

Inch—A measure of length equal of foot (1/12).

Inside The part lying within; inner side.

Jump—To move oneself suddenly from the ground.

Keeps—To withhold; continue to have or hold. To observe or pay regard to.

Lightly—With little weight, pressure or motion.

Masking Tape—An adhesive tape for covering and protecting margins, borders.

Objects—A thing that can be soon or touched. A material thing.

Other—Being the remaining one or one of two or more. Different from that or those referred to or implied.

One half _ Being single—hat; not two.

Pencil—A slender rod-shaped instrument of wood, metal; used for writing; drawing.

Picture—An image or likeness of an object, person, or scene produced on a flat surface; by painting, drawing or photography.

Plants—A living organism that unlike and animal; a young tree, shrub, ready to put in the soil.

Plastic—A factory made material that can be molded into different shapes; it is light but

Pulls—To exert force.

Punch—A sweetened drink made with fruit juices.

Remove—To move from where it is, lift, push; transfer, carry away, or from one place to another.

Rim—An edge, border or margin; the outer circular part of a wheel.

Roots—To dig into the ground the parts of plants, usually below the ground.

Set—To place in a sitting position; cause to sit.

Shake—To cause to move up and down, back and forth or from side to side with short quick movements.

Side—The right or left half a body.

Sky—The upper atmosphere.

Soak—To make thoroughly wet; drench, to put in water.

Soil—The surface layer of earth.

Space—Distance extending in all directions.

Sports—A small area of different color or texture from the main area of which it is a part.

String—A thin line of twisted fiber used for tying.

Sunlight—The light of the sun.

Third—Proceeded by two others in a series

Three—The cardinal number between two and four.

Touching—Perceive by the sense of feeling.

Toward—To the direction of.

Tray—A flat receptacle made of wood, metal, glass, plastic. Used for holding or carrying articles.

Tree—A woody perennial plant with one main stem or trunk; develops many branches.

True—To give circular motion to; to move around, or partly around.

Twelve—Four equal parts—cardinal number between eleven and thirteen.

Twenty-Four equal parts—cardinal number between nineteen and twenty-one.

Un-broked—Not broken; not disordered.

Upright—Standing, pointing or directed. Straight-up.

Upside down—With the top side underneath or turned over; disorder.

Us—We: akin to

Water—The colorless transparent liquid occurring on earth as river, lakes, oceans.

When—At what time.

Without—Not with; lacking on the outside; free from.

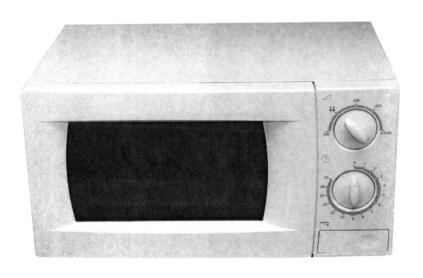

LESSON EIGHT

Title : Heat can travel.

Focus: How does heat travel best?

Vocabulary Development: Travel, heat, handles, burn, metal, wood, candles, conductor, spoon, flame, pan, pots, remove.

Materials Needed: Hand candles, matches, (adults only) metal spoon, a metal pan, a metal spoon with a wooden handle, coal, oil.

First-hand Experiment:

Directions:

> Have each student hold a metal spoon with a wooden handle over a candle flame (be careful, only hold it over the flame until the student says, "he/she feels the heat". Have the students remove the spoons immediately).
>
> Discuss with students what happened.
>
> Allow students to tell what their left and right hand felt like.

Lesson

Heat can—move from the flame through the metal spoon, but not the wooden handled one, because metal is a better conductor of heat than wood.

When something is burned, heat energy is produced. Wood, coal or oil is used mainly in factories, comes from burning coal or oil.

Heat energy is used to cook food, to warm the house on cold days, and heat water.

Can you think of other things in your home?

Vocabulary

Best—Of the most excellent sort; surpassing all others.

Better—Of a more excellent sort; more profitable.

Burn—To set on fire or subject to combustion; as in order to produce heat, light, or power.

Candles—A cylindrical mass of tallow or wax with a wick through its center, which gives light when burned.

Coal—A black combustible; mineral solid resulting from the partial decomposition of vegetable matter. A from air. A piece of glowing or charred wood, coal or similar substance.

Cook—To prepare food for eating by subjecting to heat, as by boiling, baking frying.

Conductor—A person who conduct, leader; guide; manager.

Factories—Buildings in which things are manufacturing plants.

Feels—To touch or handle in order to become aware of.

Felt—A fabric of wool, often mixed with fur or hair or with cotton, rayon.

Flame—The burning gas or vapor of a fire, seen as a flickering light of various colors; blaze.

Food—Any substance taken into and assimilated by a plant or amimal to keep alive and enable it to grow and repair tissues; nourishment.

Like—To please by agreeable to

Hand—The part of the human arm below the wrist; including the palm, fingers and thumb, used for grasping.

Handles—the part of a utensil, tool, which is to be held, turned, lifted, pulled with the hand.

Heat—The quality of being hot.

Hold—To take and keep with the hands, arms or others means; to keep from going away.

Hot—Having a high temperature, one that is higher than that of the human body.

House—A building for human beings to live in. A place that provides shelter.

Immediately—In direct contact; at the present time.

Left hand—Being on or directed toward the left.

Mainly—Chiefly; principally; in the main

Metal pan—Kitchen ware; used for cooking

Matches—Any two or more persons or things that go together in appearances, sizes, or quality; pair.

Oil—Any of various kinds of greasy, combustible substances.

Over—Above in position, outer, upper, superior; denoting a movement downward from above.

Pan—Any of many kinds of containers, usually broad, shallow, without a cover.

Pot—A round vessel of any side. Made of metal, earthenware or glass, used for holding liquids; cooking food.

Produced—To bring to view.

Remove—To move something from where it is; lift; carry away.

Right hand—Being on or directed toward the right.

Says—To utter, pronounce, or speak.

Something—A thing that is not definitely known, understood, or identified; unspecified.

Student—A person who studies.

Travel—To go from one place to another; make a journey.

Until—Up to the time of; until a specified time or occurrence.

Warm—Having or giving off a moderate degree of heat

Water—The colorless liquid occurring on earth as rivers, lakes, oceans, and falling from the clouds as rain.

Wood—A thick growth of trees. The hard, fibrous substance beneath the bark in the stems and branches of trees and shrubs.

LESSON NINE

Title: I like Bread.

Focus: Making Bread focusing on ingredients and time limit to complete.

Vocabulary Development: Materials Needed: Different colors and shapes of bread, board, dry yeast, warm water, milk, four, cloth, bowl, loaf pan, sugar, salt, soft shortening, table, oven, measuring cups.

Discussions:

What kind of bread do you like best?

When do you eat bread, and with what?

Let's get ready to make some good tasting bread:

First-hand experiences:

Directions:

Let's wash our hands and then come to the table.

Open two package of dry yeast.

Place them in the bowl.

One and three forth cups of scaled milk.

Seven; seven and one-fourth of flour, and a cloth, and a loaf pan.

Put in three tablespoons of sugar.

One teaspoon of salt.

Allow students to talk about how the bread tasted, felt and looked.

Repeat with the students what was needed to make bread.

Below is a song the students may sing and act out. It's in the tune of "Farmer in the Dell'.

The farmer grows the wheat.
The Miller grinds the flour.
The baker makes the dough.
The truck goes to the store.
The grocer's sells the bread.
The students' eat the slices.

Two tbsp. of soft shortening.

Further Directions:

Place and dissolve yeast in water.

Measure flour

Add milk

Use one half of the flour and all of the sugar, salt and shortening to the yeast

Whip until it's smooth

Put in the rest of the flour.

Place the mixture on a lightly floured board.

Place a wet cloth over the mixture for ten minutes

Knead it for ten minutes until it is smooth

Place it in a greased bowl and cover it with the cloth.

Let it rise in warm place until it doubled size (one to two hours)

Punch it down and cover it again

Let it rise again until it's almost doubled size (forty five minutes)

Now, let's make two parts and shape each into loaves

Place in a greased loaf pan

Cover it again with a cloth and let it rise until the sizes reach the top of the pan (fifty-sixty minutes)

Bake in oven at 425 degrees Fahrenheit for twenty—five minutes, or until they or dark brown

Allow them to cool then slice it for eating. You may use a spread of your choice.

Student—A person who studies.

Travel—To go from one place to another; make a journey

Until—Up to the time of; until a specified time or occurrence

Warm—Having or giving off a moderate degree of heat

Water—The colorless liquid occurring on the earth as rivers, lakes, oceans, and falling from the clouds as rain

Wood—A thick growth of trees. The hard, fibrous substance beneath the bark in the stems and branches of trees and shrubs.

Vocabulary

Almost—Very nearly but not completely

Bake—To cook food by dry heat, esp. in an oven

Baker—A person who work in a business where bread and pastry are baked

Best—Of the most excellent sort; surpassing all others most suitable, most desirables.

Bowl—A deep, rounded container or dish, open at the top

Bread—A food baked from a leavened, kneaded dough made with flour or meal, water, yeast.

Brown—Having the color of chocolate or coffee, a combination of red, black, and yellow

Farmer—A person who earns his living by farming, operates a farm.

Fifty—Five times ten—The cardinal number between forty-nine and fifty-one.

Five—The cardinal number between four and six

Flour—A fine powdery substance, produced by grinding and sifting grain, esp. What edible roasted nuts.

Forty-five—Four times ten plus five

Greased—Melted animal fat, thick oily substance.

Grind—To crush into bits between two hard surfaces, pulverize

Grocers—The food and supplies sold by a grocer.

Cloth—A woven, knitted, or pressed fabric of fibrous material, as cotton, wool, silk.

Cool—Moderately cold; neither warm nor very cold.

Cover—To place something on or over, or in front of, to conceal, protect; or close.

Doubled—Two combined; two fold, two layers; folded in two.

Dough—A mixture of flour, liquid and other ingredients, worked into a soft, thick mass for baking into a bread; pastry.

Dry—Not watery; not under water

Eat—To put food in the mouth, chew, and swallow

Grows—TO come into being or be produce naturally spring up; sprout, living

Lightly—With little weight, pressure, or motion; gentle

Loaf—A option of bread baked in one piece. Oblong shaped and in a size XXXXX

Loaves—XXXXXXXXXXXXXXXXXXXXXXXXX

Measure—The extent, dimensions, capacity, determined by a standard.

Milk—A white or yellowish liquid secreted by the mammary glands of female mammal for suckling their young

Minutes—The sixtieth part of any of certain units: 1/60 of and hour; sixty seconds

Open—In a state, which permits access, entrance, or exit, not closed

Oven—A compartment for baking or roasting food or for heating or drying things

Pan—Any of many kind s of containers, usually broad, shallow, without a cover

Parts—A portion of a whole

Punch—A sweetened drink made with fruit juices, carbonated beverages, and sherbet.

Reach—To extend

Rise—To go up to stand or assume a vertical or nearly vertical position, after sitting, kneeling, or lying

Salt—Sodium chloride, a white crystalline substance wit a characteristic taste, found natural beds in seawater: Used for seasoning food.

Skolded—A person who habitually uses abusive language

Sells—To give up, deliver or exchange. (Property, goods services) for money or its equivalent.

Shortening—Edible fat, esp. as used to make pastry, etc. crisp or flaky

Size—That quality of a thing, which determines how much space, it occupies; dimensions of a thing

Sixty—Ten times six the cardinal number between fifty-nine and sixty-one

Slice—A relatively thin piece cut from an object having some bulk or volume. A slice of an apple.

Store—To put aside, for use when needed

Sugar—Any of a class of sweet soluble, crystalline carbohydrates, as sucrose, lactose, and maltose) and monosaccharides (glucose and fructose)

Table—A thin, flat-topped piece of furniture used for people to sit down to eat on.

Taste—To test the flavor of by putting a little in one's mouth

Truck—A small wooden block

Twenty—Four equal parts—cardinal number between twenty-three and twenty-five

Until—Up to the time of occurrence

Water—The colorless liquid occurring on earth's as rivers, lakes, ocean, and falling from the cloud s as rain.

Wheat—Used for making flour

Warm—Having or giving off degree of hcat

Ycast—Any various, single, celled as comyestoos fungi: in which little or no mycelium develops and reproduce by budding; they living on sugary solutions.

LESSON TEN

Title: Living plants and animals

Focus: What must a Living plant and animal do?

Vocabulary Development:

Materials Needed: Key, crayon, plate, shade, ring, live animals, a live plant, table, fish in a fish bowl, magazines, construction paper.

First-hand experiments: If we say that something is living, what must we look for?

Directions:

Hold-up a key from the table.

Ask, if it is alive? Why?

Have the students look at the fish in the fish bowl.

Ask, is this fish alive? Why?

Lesson

A living plant and animal must eat, grow, see, hear, and breathe. If a plant and animal does not do the above things, it's not living.

Plants and animals cannot live without water

Plants and animals grow and move

Observe the fish in the bowl

What is the fish in the fish bowl doing?

Animals move more than plants. Let's go out doors to see if the plants are moving as fast as the fish in the bowl.

Further discussion by identifying pictures of living plants and animals found in a magazine, or in the room

Green plants make their own food they get water, sugar, starch for food and growth.

Draw pictures of some of the live plants and animals you saw in the magazines

Vocabulary

Animals—Any living organism except a plant or a bacterium

Bowl—A deep rounded container or dish. Open at the top

Breathe—To take (air) into the lungs and let it out but again, inhale and exhale.

Crayon—A small piece of chalk, charcoal or colored wax, used for drawing, coloring or writing.

Eat—To put (food) in the mouth chew and swallow

Fast—To abstain from all or certain food and fasting.

Fish—Any of a large group of cold blooded vertebrate animals living in water and having permanent gills for breathing, fins and usually, scales

Food—Any substance taken into and assimilated by a plant or animal to keep it alive and enable it to grow and repair tissue; nourishments, nutrients.

Grow—To come into being or be produced naturally; spring up

Hear—To perceive or sense (sounds)

Indentify—The condition of being the same or exactly alike; sameness; oneness

Living—Alive; having life; not dead

Move—To change the place or position of; push, carry

Outdoors—Any area or place outside a building or shelter.

Plants—A living organism that unlike an animal has the ability to synthesize food from carbon dioxide possesses cellulose cell walls.

See—To get knowledge or an awareness of through the eyes; perceive visually; look at esp. through stimulation of auditory nerves in the ear or sound waves/

Starch—A white tasteless, odorless food substance found in potatoes, rice, corn, wheat, cassava, and many other vegetable foods

Sugar—Any of a class of sweet soluble, crystalline carbohydrates, as sucrose, lactose, and maltose) and monosaccharides (glucose and fructose)

Table—A piece of furniture having a flat top and a set of legs

Water—The colorless liquid occurring on earth as rivers, lakes, oceans, and falling from the clouds as rain.

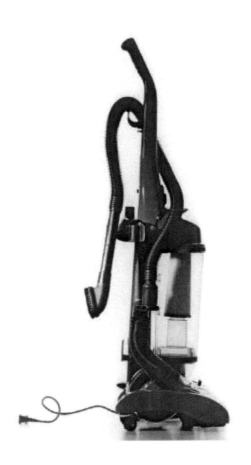

LESSON ELEVEN

Title: Machines

Focus: What are Machines?

Vocabulary Development: Pronunciations and word Meanings

Materials Needed: Vacuum, tricycle, egg beater, magazines, glue, eggs, scissors, table, empty floor space.

First-hand experiment:

Directions:

Place out the materials needed.

Explain: That a machine helps us to do work in three easy ways: By increasing the force that is used to push or pull, by increasing the speed of doing work and by changing the directions of the force.

Can you name some machines that we have here in the classroom? If so, let's find out if or which of the machines pull, push with force, changes directions or has more speed.

After their discoveries, allow students to find pictures of machines in the magazines, cut them out, and design a "Machine Corner."

Long mobile

It's the world's longest car. It stretches from Central Avenue to Orange Avenue. Once you get in it to go where you're going, you simply get out, because you're there.

or

Hickory Dickory Dock

Vocabulary

Beater—An implemented or utensil for beating

Egg—The oval or round body laid by a female bird, fish, reptile, insect, containing the germ of a new individual along with food for its development. An enclosed shell.

Empty—Containing nothing; having nothing in it.

Floor—The inside bottom surface of a room, hall, etc. on which one stands or walks

Force—Strength; energy; vigor; power

Glue—A hard, brittle gelatin made by boiling animals skins etc. to a jelly. When heated in water in forms a sticky, liquid. Used to stick things together.

Increase—To become greater in size, amount, degree etc. grow

Machine—Are used to make work easier. A device with moving parts that work together to do a job.

Push—To exert pressure or force against, esp. so as to move.

Pull—To exert force or influence on so as to cause to move toward or after the source of the force; drag to.

Scissors—A cutting instrument smaller than shears with two opposing blades, each having a looped handle, which are pivoted together in the middle so that they work against each other as the instrument is closed on the material to be cut.

Space—Distance extending in all directions.

LESSON TWELVE

Title: Magic Happening

Focus: What's Happening?

Vocabulary Development: Pronunciation and Word Meanings

Materials Needed: Popped corn, oil, lima beans, carrot seeds, see corn, navy bean seeds, radish seeds, closed fresh corn, white cotton balls, construction paper, glue, popper, pot, table, corn on the cob.

First-hand Experiment:

Do you ever ask yourself what's happening and what causes it to happen? Well, we will find out today: If you watch and listen, we will discover.

Directions:

Choose the bag that we must start with in order to get popcorn

Put a small amount of oil in pot or popper.

Place in the corn seeds. As the seeds begin to pop, ask the students what's causing them to pop. (the heat caused the water in the corn to swell up and burst). Look! How did the popping change the corn seed? (color, shape and size).

Popcorn is made from corn

Popcorn works together with corn seeds, heat, eater and oil

When it has finished popping, allow time for cooling and give the students some to eat.

(chew it well).

Use left over popcorn to create roads/numbers and letters.

Have children sing the song below. It's in the tune of "I'm a Little Tea Pot".

Heat me up, and watch me pop!
When I get all fat and white,
I'm done
Popping corn is fun!

Vocabulary

Amount—To add up; equal in total

Balls—Any round or spherical object; globe.

Beans—Any of various plants of the legume family; kidney beans, string beans, lima beans.

Carrots—A biennial plant of the parsley family, with fern like leaves and umbels of white flowers.

Causing—Anything producing an effect or result

Change—To put or take (a thing) in place of something else; substitute for; replace.

Again—Back in response; in return (answer again)

Another—One more; an additional; one of the same kind.

Away—From any given place; off; in another place, not present; absent; gone.

Bumps—To hit or knock against with a jolt; collide lightly with.

Close—Observation for time in order to see or find out something

Cloud—A visible mass of condensed water vapor suspended in the atmosphere, consisting of minute droplets or ice crystals; there are four groups.

Come—To move to a place thought of as there to or, to go into a place thought of as here, appear; to reach; enter into.

Cob—A lump or small mass; as of coal

Color—The sensation resulting from stimulation of the retina of the eye by light waves of certain lengths.

Corn—A tiny hard particle

Construction—The act or process of constructing; method of building

Cotton—Plants produce this soft white material

Direction—The act of directing; management; supervision

Discover—To be the first to find out, see or know about

Eat—To put (food in the mouth, chew, and swallow). To use up.

Fat—Containing of full of fat; oily; greasy containing volatile oil.

Find—To happen on; come upon, meet with; discover by chance; searching.

Finished—Ended; concluded

Fresh—Recently produced, obtained or grown; newly made

Fun—Lively, gay play, amusement, sports, recreation, pleasure

Glue—A hard, brittle gelatin made by boiling animal skins etc. to a jelly. When heated in water it forms a sticky, liquid. Used to stick things together.

Happening—To take place; occurred; bxxxxxxxxxxxxxx Without plan

Heat—The quality of being hot

Little—Small in size; not big, large pr great

Magazines—Publications with a paper back and contains stories, articles.

Magic—The use of charms, spells and XXXXXX in seeking or pretending or cause or central—events; or govern certain natural or supernatural forces; sorcery; witchcraft.

Order—Social position rank in the community. The sequence or arrangement of things or events; series; succession

Paper—A think flexible material made usually in sheets from a pulp prepared from rags, wood, or other fibrous material, used for writing or printing on

Table—A piece of furniture having a flat top and a set of legs.

Together—In or into one gathering; group, mass, or place

Water—The colorless liquid occurring on earth as rivers, lakes, oceans, and falling from the clouds as rain.

What—Which thing, event circumstances used interrogatively in asking for the specification of an identity, quantity, quality.

Work—Physical or mental effort exerted to do or make something; purposeful activity.

Pot—A round vessel of any size, made of metal, earthenware, or glass, used for holding liquids, cooking or preserving food.

Radish—An annual plant of the mustard family, with an edible root.

Seeds—The part of a flowering plant that typically contains the embryo with protective cast and stored food and will develop into a new plant if sown; fertilize and let mature.

Shape—The finished form in which something may appear

Size—A thing which determines how much shape it covers

Speed—The act or state of moving rapidly, quick motion.

Surprise—Come upon suddenly at unexpectedly; take unawares.

LESSON THIRTEEN

Title: Molds

Focus: What are Molds?

Vocabulary Development: Pronunciation and Word Meaning

Materials Needed: Two slices of white bread, table, water, bowl, plastic wrap, magnifying glass, garbage bags, paper marker, rubber band, crayon, a clock and a camera.

First-hand Experimental:

Directions:

Place two slices of white bread on a table for an hour sprinkle each piece with a few drops of water.

Put them in the bowl and cover with the plastic wrap

Put them in a warm place away from direct sunlight

Check them daily for seven days

After the seventh day, remove the plastic wrap

Use the magnifying glass to see what's happening

Take pictures

After two weeks, place the bread in plastic bags to get a closer look

Look at the bread you will see spots of different sizes and colors.

Each day, the spots grow bigger

Give the children construction paper and crayons to draw pictures of bread that they should not eat.

Vocabulary

Bigger—Of great size, extend; great in force or intensity

Bowl—A deep rounded container, open at the top

Bread—A food baked from leavened, kneaded dough made with flour or meal, water, yeast

Closer—Shut; not open

Cobweb—A web spun by a spider

Color—The sensation resulting from stimulation of the retina of the eye by light waves of certain lengths

Cover—To place something on or cover, or in front of, to conceal, protect; or close

A hard brittle substance usually transparent or translucent made by fusing silicates with soda, lime and sometimes various metallic oxide.

Green—Of the color that is characteristic of growing grass

Grow—To come into being or be produced

Happening—Something that happens; occurrence; incident; event

Lumps—A solid mass of lump. No special shape one small enough to be taken up in the hand, hunk. To become lumpy.

Magnifier—A person who magnify to make greater in size, status, enlarge.

Marker—A person or thing that marks; a device for keeping scores, marking lines, a bookmark

Different—Not alike, dissimilar, separate

Direct—By the shortest way: without turning or stopping; not round about

Drops—A small quantity of liquids that is somewhat spherical or pear shaped, as when falling.

Dusty—Covered with dust; full of dust; powdery

Eat—To put (food) in the mouth, chew, and swallow

Fuzzy—Of like, or covered with fuzz

Glass—An article made portly or wholly of glass as a drinking container, mirror, windowpane, telescope.

Mold—A downy of furry growth on the surface of organic matter; caused by fungi esp. in the presence of dampness or decay

Never—Never not ever; at no time; not at all

Piece—A part of fragment broken or separated from the whole

Place—A short, narrow, street, space, room, naturally, spring up, sprout.

Plastic—A factory made material that can be molded into different

Remove—To move (something) from where its is; lift, push, transfer, or carry away

Seven—The cardinal number between six and eight

Should—Part of shall. An auxiliary used to express, obligation, duty, necessity.

Size—That quality of a thing which determines how much space it occupies; dimensions or magnitude of a thing

Slices—A relatively thin, broad piece cut from an object having some bulk or volume, (a slice of apple).

Spots—A small area of different color of texture from the main area of which it is a part; stain, speck, patch.

Sprinkle—To scatter water in drops or particles upon; cover, dampen

Sunlight—The light of the sun

Table—A thin, flat tablet or slab of metal, stone; or wood, used for inscriptions, (a piece of furniture usually set on legs. We set with food for a meal.

Two—The cardinal number between one and three

Water—The colorless, transparent liquid occurring on earth as rivers, lakes, oceans, and falling from the clouds as rain.

Weeks—A period of seven days

Wrap—To wind for fold (a covering) around something

LESSON FOURTEEN

Title: The Moon

Focus: What is the Moon?

Vocabulary Development: Pronunciations and Word Meanings

Materials Needed: Globe, a picture of the moon, pictures of the phases of the moon, glue, overhead projector, construction paper, crayons, a pan, cotton water, flash light, magnet.

Have you ever looked up in the sky at night and there was something up there that was very bright in the night sky. **It might have looked like a ball, but not all moons look around, nor does it appear in the same place in the sky**.

Lesson

The moon is the earth's satellite, because it revolves around the earth.

The moon does not give off its own light. It catches the light from the sun, and it bounces back to earth. Animals and plants do not breathe or live on the moon.

The moon's gravitational pulling causes oceans to rise and fall, which are known as tides (high, low).

First-hand Experiment:

Directions:

Demonstrate why the moon is the earth's satellite

Demonstrate the position of the moon, earth and sun. Which one is closer to earth?

Use the overhead projector to demonstrate how the moon catches light from the sun and it bounces back to earth.

Use magnet to demonstrate gravitational holding or pulling

Use a pan to show a high tide and a low tide

Factual discussion

Allow students to draw the phases of the moon posted on your chart paper.

Sample

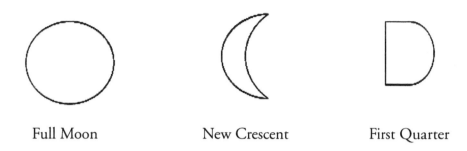

Full Moon   New Crescent   First Quarter

Use cotton to create the phases of the moon. Students may learn "moon-come-out".

Moon-Come-Out

Moon-come-out
And sun-go in
Here's a soft blanket
To cuddle your chin

Moon-Go-In
And sun-come-out
Throw off the blanket
And bustle about

Or when night is dark
My cat is wise
To light the lanterns
In his eyes
By: Alleen Fisher

Taken from *Read-Aloud Rhymes for the Very Young*.

Vocabulary

Animals—Any living organism except a plant or bacterium.

Around—Round; in a circle

Bounces—To bump or thump; to cause to hit against a surface so as to spring back

Breathe—To take air into the lungs and let it out again, inhale and exhale.

Bright—Shining with light that is radiated or reflected: Full of light

Close—Shut, not open

Construction—The act or process of constructing; building

Crayon—A small piece of chalk, charcoal or colored wax, used for drawing, coloring or writing

Demonstrate—To explain or make clear by using examples, experiments

Different—Not alike dissimilar, separate

Earth—The planet that we live on

Flash light—A portable electric light, usually operated by batteries

Globe—Circular representation of the earth; including boundaries.

Gravitational—The act, process, or fact of gravitating; a force that tends to draw all bodies in the earth's sphere toward the center of the earth.

Known—pp of known to have a clear understanding

Light—To shine bright

Magnet—A thing that attracts

Moon—The earth's only natural satellite, which revolves around a planet

Night—The period from sunset to sunrise the period of darkness after sunset.

Overhead Projector—A machine used to direct pictures or objects on a screen.

Pan—Any of many kinds of containers, usually broad, shallow, without a cover, and made of metal, used for domestic purposes

Paper—A thing flexible material in sheets made from rags, wood, pulp etc.

Phases—Some of the forms of the moon

Place—A particular area or locality; region, the part of space occupied by a thing; situation.

Plant—A living organism that has the ability to synthesize food from carbon dioxide, process of cellulose cell walls and lacks centrosomes, specialized sense organs, and digestive nervous and circulatory systems. Young trees, shrubs or herb, ready to put into other soil for growth maturity.

Pulling—To exert force or influence on so as to cause to move toward or after the source of the force; drag, tug, draw.

Revolves—To cause to rotate, or spin around a point.

Same—A like
Satellite—Something that circles the planets

Sky—The upper atmosphere; reference to its appearance, blue skies, cloudy skies

Sun—The self-luminous, gaseous sphere about which the earth and other planets revolve and which furnishes light, heat and energy for the solar system, it is the star nearest the earth.

Tide—The altenate rise and fall of the surface of oceans, seas, bays and rivers. Connected with the caused by attraction as the moon and sun, current.

Water—The colorless liquid occurring an earth as rivers, lakes, oceans, and falling from the clouds as rain.

LESSON FIFTEEN

Title: Rain

Focus: Water is Rain?

Vocabulary Development: Pronunciation and Word Meanings

Materials Needed: Jar, water, top to close jar.

First-hand Experiment: Rain forms inside of clouds especially those that are dark and gray colors

Lesson

There are many, many droplets of water inside a cloud. Which bumps in to each other, and form larger drops. When the drops are big enough, they fall from the clouds as rain.

The sun's heat takes water from the land, rivers and seas. Water rises into the air as water vapor then comes back down onto the land, rivers and seas. No new water is ever made.

Experiment Directions:

Fill a large jar half way with water.

Cover it tightly

Place the jar in direct sunlight

Watch the droplets run down the sides and into the water. The water in the jar becomes water vapor.

Discuss what happened

Take pictures

Allow students to use construction paper and crayons to create their rain, coming from the clouds. You may use cotton clouds.

Take students outdoors to see the different kinds of clouds. However, if it's a rainy day, have the students say:

Rain, rain, go away, come again another day!

Rain Poem

The rain was like a little mouse, quiet, small and gray
It pattered all around the house and then it went away
It did not come, I understand, indoors at all until it found
an open window and left tracks across the sill.
                    By: Elizabeth Coatsworth

Or Snap

She was opening up her umbrella she thought it was going to rain. When we all heard a snap. Like the clap of a trap and we never have seen her again.

Vocabulary

Again—back in response; in return (answer again)

Another—One more; an additional; one of the same kind.

Away—From any given place; off; in another place; not present; absent; gone

Bumps—To hit or knock against with a jolt; collide lightly with.

Close—Observation for a time in order to see or find out something

Clouds—A visible mass of condensed water vapor suspended in the atmosphere, consisting of minute droplets or ice crystals: there are four groups.

Come —To move to a place thought of as "there" to or to go into a place thought of as here; appear; to reach; enter into.

Dark—Entirely or partly without light, neither giving not receiving light.

Day—The period of light, between sunrise and sunset

Direct—By the shortest way, without turning or stopping; not round about straight.

Down—From a higher or lower place toward the ground.

Droplets—A very small drops

Drops—A small quantity of liquid that is somewhat spherical or pear shaped, as when

Falling—To come down because detached, pushed; dropped; to come down suddenly

Forms—The shape, outline, or configuration of anything; structure as apart from color, material a model esp. one used to display or fit clothes

Go—To move along, proceed; to move about or be in a certain condition or state

Grey—A color

Half—Either of the two equal parts of something

Happened—To take place, occurred; befall

Heat—The quality of being hot, great warmth.

Inside—The part lying within; inner side, surface, or part, interior.

Jar—A container made of glass, stone, or ear then ware, with a large opening and not spout; partly open.

Land—The solid part of the earth's surface not covered by water.

Large—Generous, big, great, taking up much space.

Made—Constructed, shaped; formed, invented, prepared.

New—Never existing before appearing made, produced.

Rain—Water falling to earth in drops that have been condensed from the moisture in the atmosphere.

Rainy—Bringing rain

Rivers—A natural stream of water larger than a creek and emptying into an ocean, a lake, or another river.

Run—To go by moving the legs rapidly; faster than walking, in such a way that for an instant both feet are off the ground.

Seas—The continous body of salt water covering they rather part of the earth's surface; ocean

Sun—The self-luminous, gaseous sphere about which the earth and other planets revolve and which furnishes light, heat, and energy for the solar system, it is the star nearest the earth.

Sunlight—The light of the sun.

Top—The upper or highest part, section, point, or surface of anything.

Vapor—Visible particles of moisture floating in the air, as fog, mist, or steam.

LESSON SIXTEEN

Title: Rainbows

Focus: What is a rainbow?

Vocabulary Development: Pronunciations and word meanings

Materials Needed: a prism. A sunny room with shades or blinds, a wall, table, construction paper, crayons, cellophane, over head projector.

First-hand Experiment:

Directions:

Show the students a prism

Ask students to tell what shape it is, and what kind of material it is made of.

Pull down the shades with a narrow amount of sunshine coming in.

Darken the room

Place the prism into the sunlight or over overhead projector light

Look!

Have the students tell the colors they see in the rainbow. How many?

Where do we see rainbows, when we are out doors?

Use cellophane to see if we can get one color from the prism.

Allow students to draw and color their own rainbow in the right color order

Factual discussion.

Explain to students that rainbow show-up when the sun's rays are sent by passing raindrops.

Take pictures and use the students' creations in the "Rainbow Center"

Vocabulary

Amount—To add up; equal in total

Cellophane—A thin transparent material form cellulose used as moisture proof; wrapping for feed, tobacco

Color—The sensation resulting from stimulation of the retina of the eye by light waves of certain lengths.

Crayon—A small piece of chalk, charcoal or colored wax, used for drawing, coloring or writing.

Draw—To make move toward one or along with one by or as by exerting force; pull, to pull-up. A drawing or something being drawn.

Narrow—Small in width as compared to length, standard; not wide

Order—The sequence of arrangement of things or events; series; succession.

Outdoor—Any area or place outside a building or shelter

Passing—Going by; beyond, past; over or through

Pictures—An image or likeness of an object. Person, or scene produced on a flat surface esp. by painting, drawing, or photography.

Prism—A solid figure whose ends are parallel, polygonal, and equal in size and shape; and whose sides are parallelograms.

Projector—A machine for throwing image on a screen.

Rainbow—Containing the colors of the spectrum in consecutive bands; formed in the sky by the refraction, reflection, and _____ of the sun's ray in falling rain or on _____ many colors.

Rays—Any of the thin lines or beams of light that appear to come from a bright source.

Right—Not curved; straight; designation are the corresponding side of anything; correct; good, proper

Shades—A definite area of shade cast upon surface by a body intercepting the light rays

Sunny—Sunlight; full of sunshine

Sunshine—The shining of the sun; light and hear from the sun

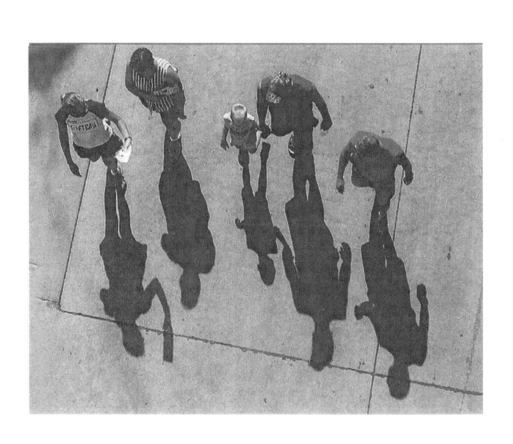

LESSON SEVENTEEN

Title: Shadows

Focus: What is a shadow?

Vocabulary Development: Pronunciation and word meanings.

Materials Needed: Crayons, construction paper, overhead projector, board

Shadows are created by some person, animal or thing. A partly dark place.

Lesson

Some times your shadow is much larger than you are, and at other times it is shorter.

The earth and the moon passes through each other's shadow five to seven times each year. In the darkest part of the shadow, you cannot see the sun. The sun has been overshadowed by the moon. This happens during the daylight.

First-hand Experiments:

Directions:

Make shadows on the over-head projector.

Draw a moon

Draw a complete over shadowing of the moon (a total eclipse)

Find shadows indoors and outdoors

An example of a computer over shadowing of the moon (a total eclipse)

Reflections

"Each time I see the upside down man standing in the water.
I look at him and start to laugh, although I shouldn't oughter.
For maybe in another world another time. Another town
Maybe he is right side up, and I am upside down."

By Shel Silverstein

Vocabulary

Animal—Any living organism except a plant or bacterium

Complete—Lacking no component part; full whole finished

Construction—The act or process of constructing; building

Crayon—A small stick of chalk, charcoal, or colored wax; used for drawing, coloring, or writing

Darkest—Entirely without light

During—Through out the entire time of, all through

Earth—The planet that we live on.

Eclipse—A partial or total observing of the sun when the moon comes between it and the earth called the solar eclipse.

Indoors—In a house or other building

Large—Generous; big; great

Moon—The heavenly body that revolves around the earth from west to east

Over—In, at, or to a position up from; higher; than; across-and down

Overhead—Located or operating above the level of the head; designating a door, a garage.

Paper—A thin flexible material made usually in sheets from a pulp prepared from rags, wood or other fibrous materials, used for writing or printing on.

Person—A human being

Prizm—A solid figure whose ends are parallel, polygomal, and equal in size and shape; and whose sides are parallelograms.

Projector—A machine for throwing and image on a screen.

Shadow—A definite area of shade cast upon a surface by a body intercepting, the light rays.

Shorter—Not extending far from end to end not long.

Sometimes—At some time not known or specified.

Sunshine—The shining of the sun; the light and heat from the sun

Total—Constituting the whole, entire amount

Year—A period of 365 days (in leap year) 366 days divided into twelve months beginning January 1 and ending December 31

LESSON EIGHTEEN

Title: Sounds

Focus: What is Sound?

Vocabulary Development: Pronunciation and word meanings.

Materials Needed: Glass, wall or door, ear, code, water, sand, jar with covers

Sounds moves at different speeds through different materials.

Sounds moves faster through water than through air.

First-hand Experiment:

Directions:

Hold an empty glass (with care) against the door on the other side near the sound.

Carefully put your ear against the bottom part of the glass.

Allow someone to tap on the other door from far away. What happened?

Make up a code. (clap 1,2,3 etc)

Discuss what you heard.

Lesson

The vibrating wall or door shakes the air inside the glass and the sounds
are passed to your ear

Use a different type of material, water, jar, sand jar with a closed cover.
What happened?

Redirect factual information

Music Career

She wanted to play the piano
But her hands couldn't reach the keys
Her feet couldn't reach the floor
When her hands could finally reach the keys
And her feet could reach the floor
She didn't want to play that ol' piano anymore

Vocabulary

Against—In opposition to; contrary to

Bottom—The lowest part

Clap—To make a sudden, explosive sound as of two flat surfaces being struck together.

Code—A body of laws, any set principles or rules of conduct.

Cover—To place something on, over, or in front of to conceal, protect or close.

Different—Not alike; dissimilar

Door—A movable structure for opening or closing an entrance; as to a building, a room, of giving access to a closet.

Ear—The part of the body specialized for that perception of sound; organ of hearing

Empty—Containing nothing; having nothing in it.

Glass—A hard brittle substance usually transparent or translucent, made by fusing silicates with soda or potash, lime and land sometimes various metallic oxides.

Heard—To perceive or sense sounds; through simulation of auditory nerves in the ear by sounds waves.

Jar—A container made of glass, stone or earthen ware, with a large opening and no spoal

Moves—To change the place or position of push, carry or pull from one position to another.

Passed—To go or move forward through or out; to extend, lead; to go by

Sand—Loose, gritty particles of worn of disintergrated rock varying in size, deposited along the shores of bodies of water.

Shake—To cause to move up and down, back and forth, or from side to side with short, quick movements

Sound—Free form defect, damage; or decay whole and in good condition; vibrations in air, water that stimulates the auditory sensation produced by seen vibrations.

Speed—The act or state of moving rapidly; swiftness, quick motion.

Tap—To strike something lightly, repeatedly.

Through—In one side and out of the other side of; from end to end of

Vibrating—The action of vibrating; movement back and forth as of a pendulum; rapid rhythmic movement.

Wall—An upright structure of wood stone, brick; serving to enclose, divide, support or protect.

Water—The colorless, transparent liquid occurring on earth as rivers, lakes, oceans and falling from the clouds as rain.

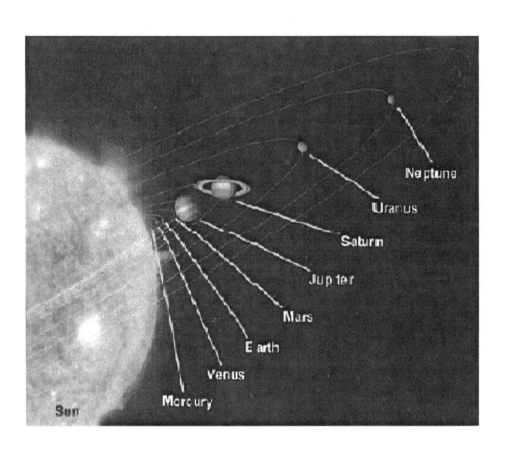

LESSON NINETEEN

Title: Sun's Family

Focus: Who is the Sun's Family?

Vocabulary Development: Pronunciation and word meanings.

Materials Needed: Chart (family) construction paper, crayons, board, and a solar system chart.

Just as you have a family, the sun has a family too, the solar system.

Lesson

There are nine sisters and brothers that moves around the sun.

Look at the chart on the board, the solar system.

Can you find the planet earth on the chart?

We live on the planet earth.

The sun is the biggest family member, and it holds all the family members in place by gravity, (a pulling force).

First-hand Experiment:

Directions:

> Let's look at the chart of the names of the sun's family
>
> Point and day the names and have students repeat them
>
> Have students identify the first letter of each sun's family name
>
> Have students tell if their name begins with the same first letter as a sun's family member's name
>
> Write the student's name next to the sun's family name
>
> Ask the students to give the names of their family and friends that begins with the first letter of the sun's family names.

Lesson

Mercury is the closet family member to the sun

It takes many years for each of the sun's family to move around the sun

Allow students to draw pictures of their family members and write any sun's family names that begins like their family names (P,U,J,S,N,V,M,E,P,M)

Create: "My family Corner"

Vocabulary

Around—Round in a circle, on all sides in every direction

Begins—To start doing, acting, going; get under way

Biggest—Of great size, extent, or capacity; large a great in force or intensity.

Board—A long, broad, flat piece of sawed wood ready for use; thin plank

Brothers—A boy or man related to other children of his parents; a parent in common.

Chart—A group about facts about something; set up in the form of a diagram table; graph.

Construction—The act or process of constructing

Crayons—A small stick of chalk, charcoal or colored wax, used for drawing, coloring, writing

Draw—To move toward one thing or along with one by or as by exerting force, pull, haul, drag.

Earth—The planet that we live on.

Family—All people living in the same house; household.

First—Preceeding all others in a series; before any others; 1ˢᵗ; used as the ordinal of one.

Force—Strength, energy; vigor, power

Friend—A person whom one knows well and is fond of; close, associate, acquaintance

Gravity—Of or caused by gravitation force that tends to draw all bodies in the earth's sphere toward the center of the earth.

Holds—To take and keep with the hands, or other means; grasp, clutch; seize; to keep from going away.

Identify—The condition of being the same or exactly alike; sameness; oneness

Letter—A symbol or character to represent a speech sound or sounds. Alphabets.

Longest—Measuring much from end to end in space or from beginning to end in time; not short or brief

Members—A part or organ of a human or animal body; an arm or leg

Mercury—The smallest planet in the solar system and the ones nearest the sun.

Moves—To change the place or position of; push, carry or pull from one place to another.

Next—In the time, place, degree or rank nearest or immediately proceeding or following

Pictures—An image or likeness of an object, person, or scene produced or flat surface; painting, drawing, or photography.

Planet—Any of the heavenly bodies with apparent motion (as distinguished from the fixed stars.

Repeat—To say or utter against; reiterate;

Same—Being the very one; identical; alike; in kind; quality; amount or degree

Sisters—A woman or girl as she is related to the other children of her parents

Solar—Having to with the sun

Sun—The self—luminous, gaseous sphere about which the earth and other planets revolve and which furnishes light, heat, and energy, for the solar system; it is the star nearest the earth.

System—A set or arrangement of things so related or connected as to form a unity or organic whole.

Think—To form or have in the mind conceive thoughts; opinion.

Years—A period of 365 days (in leap years 366 days) divided into 12 months, beginning January 1 and ending December 31

LESSON TWENTY

Title: Water

Focus: What are the five largest bodies of water?

Vocabulary Development: Pronunciation and word meanings.

Materials Needed: Plastic bottles, water, camera, measuring cup, blue food coloring, vegetable oil, cap for bottles, globe.

Can you think of what we need water for?

Lesson

All live plants and animals have to have water in order to live.

Today we will recognize the location of five large bodies of water; the Atlantic, Pacific, Indian, Arctic and Antartica Oceans.

Half of the people in the country lives near oceans. Two-thirds of our earth's water is ice.

First-hand Experiments:

Directions:

Fill a one-half liter clear plastic bottle half with one cup of water.

Add four drops of blue food coloring.

Carefully, pour in one cup of vegetable oil.

Place the cap tightly on

Rock your ocean in the bottle (back and forth)

Watch the waves on the ocean

Discuss, and take pictures.

Allow students to draw pictures of an ocean, indicating or including waves, planets and animals that lives in the ocean.

Explain: Water is the liquid that fill the oceans, rivers, lakes and ponds, that falls from the sky as rain.

What, and how do we use water?

Vocabulary

Animals—Any living organism except a plant or bacterium

Antartica—Land area about the South Pole completely covered by an ice shelf, something called a continent

Arctic—Of characteristic of or near the North Pole or the region around it, very cold.

Atlantic—An ocean touching the American continents to the West and Europe and Africa in the east, greatest known depth.

Bodies—Any of the natural objects seen in the visible heaven the sun, moon, planets and stars

Bottle—A container for liquids usually made of glass, earthenware of plastic and having a relatively narrow neck.

Carefully—Acting or working thoughtful, painstaking way

Clear—Free from clouds or mist bright, light

Color—The sensation resulting form stimulation of the retina of the eye by light waves of certain lengths

Cup—A small, open container for beverages, bowl-shaped and with a handle

Drops—A small quantity of liquid that is somewhat spherical or pear-shaped; as when falling

Fall—To come down by the force of gravity; drop, descend, pushed, dropped

Five—The cardinal number between four and six

Food—Any substance taken into and assimilated by a plant or animal to keep it alive and enable it to grow and repair tissue; nourishment

Four—The cardinal numbers totaling one more than three.

Ice—The glassy, brittle, crystalline form of water made solid by cold; frozen water

Include—To shut up or in; enclose

Indian—A member of any of the aboriginal people of North America

Indicating—To direct attention to; point to r point out; show

Lake—An inland body of usually fresh water, larger than a pool or pond; generally formed by some obstruction in the courage of flowing water.

Largest—Generous, big, great, taking up much space.

Liquid—Readily flowing; fluid, unlike a solid.

Lives—Having life; not dead

Location—A locating or being located, position in space.

Measuring—The extent, dimensions, capacity of anything; as determined by a standard measurement.

Oceans—The great body of salt water that covers approximately 71% of the surface of the earth.

Pacific—The largest of the earth's oceans

People—All the persons of a racial, National religion, or linquistic, group, nation race.

Picture—An image or likeness of an object, person or scene produced on a flat surface, by painting, drawing, or photography

Plants—A living organism that has the ability to synthesize food from carbon dioxide, possesses, cellulose cell wall and lacks centrosomes specialized sense organs and digestive nervous and circulatory systems.

Plastic—Molding or shaping matter; formative

Ponds—A body of standing water smaller

Pour—To flow freely; continuously (put in)

Rain—Water falling to earth in drops that have been condensed from the moisture in the atmosphere.

Recognize—To be aware of something or someone known before or as the same as that known

Rivers—A natural stream of a water larger than a creek and emptying into an ocean, a lake or another river

Rock—Move or sway; back and forth; a strong rocking motion

Sky—The upper atmosphere, with reference to its appearance.

Lightly—No close or compact in structure that water, air; cannot pass through

Vegetable—Of or having the nature of plants in general; consisting of or produced by, edible vegetables.

Watch—The act of keeping alert, in order to look after, protect, guard

Water—The colorless, transparent liquid occurring on earth as rivers, lakes, oceans and falling from the clouds as rain.

LESSON TWENTY-ONE

Title: Weather

Focus: What is weather?

Vocabulary Development: Pronunciation and word meaning.

Materials Needed: Glass, flashlight, water, small pans, string, strong cardboard, sink, globe, thermamenter, magazines, glue, scissors, cups, table.

Lesson

Weather is a condition of the atmosphere, at a given place, at a certain time. It includes air temperature, air pressure, moisture in the air, and the speed and direction of the winds, which change from day to day.

The sun is the main cause of our weather conditions.

Air is called our atmosphere.

When you were on your way to school today, did you notice if it was sunny, cloudy, hot, or cold?

Air is all around us. We can't see it. We can feel it when it blows. We can hear it as it blows branches on the trees. Yet, we must have air to breathe.

Many areas are affected due to a change in the weather.

Doctors know that seasonal changes are responsible for breathing conditions (respiratory)

Business activities are affected

Vocabulary

Activities—The quality or state of being active; action

Affects—To make a pretense of being, having, feeling, liking

Air—The elastic, invisible mixture of gases that surrounds the earth; atmosphere.

Antarctica—Land area about the South Pole, completely covered by an ice shelf

Around—Round; in a circle; along a circular course or circumference

Atmosphere—The gaseous envelope (air) surrounding the earth.

Blows—To move with some force; said of the wind or a current of air.

Branches—Any woody extension growing from the trunk or main stem or from a main limb of a tree

Breathe—To take air into the lungs and let it out again; inhale, exhale

Bureau—An agency for collecting and giving information or performing other services

Business—One's work, occupation; or profession

Cardboard—A material made of paper pulp but thicker and stiffer than paper; posterboard used for making cards and boxes.

Cause—Anything producing an effect or result.

Certain—Fixed, settled, or determined

Changes—To put or take (a thing) in place of something else.

Clothing—Wearing apparel; clothes, garments

Cloudy—Covered with clouds; overcast

Cold—Of temperature much lower than that of human body, very chilly

Condition—Anything that modifies or restricts the mature, existence, or occurrence of something else.

Cube—A solid with six equal, square sides

Cup—A small, open container for beverages, usually bowl-shaped and with a handle

Dark—Entirely or partly without light

Degree—Any of the successive steps or stages in a process or series.

Directly—In direct way or line straight; without a person or thing coming between.

Directions—Instructions for doing, operating, using, preparing, order or command.

Doctors—A person on whom a university or college has conferred one of its highest degrees after fulfilled academic requirements.

Equipment—Special things needed for some purpose; supplies, furnishings, apparatus.

Etheopia—County in East Africa, on the Red Sea
Farenheit—

Feel—To touch or handle in order to become aware of; examines or test by touching

Fill—To much as possible into; make full.

Forecasters—A person who make predictions as of weather conditions

Freezing—To be formed into ice; be hardened or solidified by cold.

Glass—A hard brittle substance usually transparent, made by fusing silicates with soda or potash, lime and sometimes various metallic oxides.

Hear—To perceive or sense (sounds), through stimulation of auditory nerves in the ear by sounds waves.

Hot—Having a high temperature; one that is higher than that of the human body

Hurricanes—A violent tropical cyclone with winds moving at 73 or more miles per often torrential rains

Ice—The glassy, brittle, crystalline form of water made solid by cold frozen water.

Identify—To make identical, consider or treat as the same

Includes—To shut up or in; enclose; to have as part of a whole

Information—An informing or being told of something

Kept—pp. of keep; to pay regard for

Leaves—To cause or allow to remain, not to take away.

Light—Having little weight the form of electromagnetic radiation that act upon the retina of the eye, making sight possible.

Globe—Any round ball-shaped thing sphere; a spherical model of the earth showing the continents, sea.

Magazine—A publications; usually with a paper back and sometimes illustrated, that at regular intervals and contains stories articles.

Main—The principal or most important part or point

Minus—Reduced by the subtraction of; less than

Moving—Changing; or causing to change place; or position

Must—Compulsion, obligation, requirement of necessity

Night—The period from sunset to sunrise

Ninety—Four the cardinal number between eighty-nine and ninety-five

Official—Of or holding an office or position of authority

Outdoors—Any area or place outside a building or shelter.

Over—Above in position, outer, upper superior, eminent; passing across or beyond

Owns—Belonging, relating or peculiar to oneself or itself

Pan—Any of many kinds of containers usually broad, shallow, without a cover, and made of metal used for domestic purposes

Parts—A portion or division of a whole

Path—a line of movement, course taken

Perishable—Liable to spoil or deteriorate, as some foods.

Pictures—An image or likeness of an object, person or scene produced on a flat surface; by painting, drawing or photography

Press—To action with steady force or weight; push steadily against

Pressure—A pressing or being pressed; compression; squeezing

Pushed—To exert pressure or force against move it; to move forward

Records—To put in writing, print, for future use.

Responsibiltiy—Condition, quality, fact; or instance of being responsible

Return—To go or come back as to a former place, condition, practice, opinion.

Seasonal—Characteristics of, or depending on the season

See—To get knowledge or an awareness of through the eyes, perceive visually look at

Seventy—Seven times ten; the cardinal number between sixty-nine and seventy-one

Shines—To emit or reflect light, be radiant or bright with light; to make shinny

Shipping—The act of business of sending or transporting goods.

Sink—To go beneath the surface of water descend, partly or completely under sunk

Small—Little in size when compared with others at the same kind; not large or big

Speed—The act or state of moving rapidly; swiftness

Square—A plane figure having four equal sides and four right angles

State—A set of circumstances of attributes characterizing a person or thing at a given times

Station—The place where a person or thing stands or is located.

Storms—An atmosphere disturbance characterized by a storm wind; usually accompanied by rain, snow, sleet, or hail; and often thunder and lightening

Strong—A physically, powerful, having great muscular strength; robust

Sun—The self-luminous, gaseous sphere about which the earth and other planets revolve and furnishes light, heat energy for the solar system.

Sunny—Shining or bright with sunlight; full of sunshine

Temperature—The degree of hotness or coldness of anything

Thermonentor—An instrument for measuring temperature consisting of a graduated glass tube with a seale, capillary bore in which mercury colored alcohol

Thirty-two—The cardinal number between twenty-nine and thirty-one

Thunderstorms—To strike, drive, attack with the sound or violence of thunder. A storm accompanied by thunder and lighting

Tornado—A violently whirling column of air extending downward from a cummulonmbus cloud, rapidly, rotating, slender, funnel-shaped that usually destroys everything along its narrow path.

Tree—A woody perennial plant with one main stem or trunk which develops many branches, usually at some height above the ground.

Turn—To move about a central point or axis; revolve or rotate
Upside down—With the top side or part underneath or turned over inverted

Very—In the fullest sense; complete; absolute

Warmest—Having or giving off a moderate degree of heat

Way—A means of passing from one place to another; as a road, highway, street path

Weather—The general condition of the atmosphere at a particular time and place with regard to the temperature moisture, cloudiness

Winds—Air in motion; any noticeable natural movement of air parallel to the earth's surface

World—On earth or in the universe, anywhere at all; ever

LESSON TWENTY-TWO

Title: Soil that holds the most water

Focus: What soil holds the most water?

Vocabulary Development: Pronunciation and word meanings.

Materials Needed: Three one liter plastic bottles (without caps); three, two cups (four-hundred ml) jars with mouth smaller than the width of the plastic bottles, three types of soil. (clay, sand and loam) and old nylon stocking, string or rubber bands, masking tape, sharp knife (adults only) measuring cup, scissors, water and camera; timer

In this lesson, we will discover which soil holds the most water for the longest period of time

First-hand Experiment:

Directions:

> Adult: Cut the bottom of each plastic bottle, one inch from the bottom, then use the scissors to finish cutting the bottom off

> Cut three pieces out of the old stocking large enough to cover the mouth of each bottle. Use the rubber bands to hold the stockings in place.

> Fill one bottle with three quarters of clay another bottle with sand, and the third bottle with loam

Place three pieces of tape around the rim of each jar (spaced apart equally)

Add three layers of tape over the first layer to keep the air from getting out of the bottles

Put each plastic bottles mouth down into a jar

Pour eight ounces of water into each kind of soil

Check the time when you poured the water in

Watch to see what happens

Preparation discussion

Questions:

What kind of soil left the most amount of water? Or the least amount of water? Clay, sand or loam?

Sand drained faster and left the most amount of water

Lesson

The clay was the slowest in draining the water

Loam, is both sand and clay, plus other materials, so it is a medium drainer.

When the water was poured on the sand, it pushed the air out of the way and quickly moved through the sand

Clay particles are much smaller than sand, so there is less room between them for the water to move

It takes a lot of time because the tiny spaces, clay does drain slower

Clay holds water. It keeps the water it has. It stays without the longest. It's a good mud maker.

Loam is the best soil for growing plants

Take pictures

Draw a simple bar graph.

Vocabulary

Adults—Grown-up; mature; in age, size, strength

Air—The elastic, invisible mixture of gases that surrounds the earth; atmosphere

Amount—To add up; equal in total

Around—Round; in a circle; along a circular course or circumference

Because—For the reason or cause that; and account of the fact that; since

Best—Of the most excellent sort; surpassing all others

Between—In or through the space that separates (two things)

Both—The two, the one and the other together, equally; as well, used correlatively; with

Bottle—A container for liquids usually made of glass, earthenware, or plastic, with a narrow neck

Cap—Any close fitting head covering

Check—To investigate in order to determine the condition, validity

Clay—A firm, fine-grained earth, plastic when wet, composed of hydrous aluminum silicates minerals its is produced by the chemical decomposition of rocks in water used for bricks pottery

Cup—A small open container for beverages, bowl shaped and with a handle

Cutting—The act of one that cuts a clipping

Down—From a higher to a lower place

Drained—To draw off liquids gradually

Enough—As much or as often as necessary

Faster—Rapidly, swiftly, quickly, speedily

Fill—To put as much as possible into; make full

Getting—To come into the state of having; receiver, gain obtain

Graph—Something that writes or records, something written

Growing—To come into being or produced naturally, spring up, sprout

Hold—To take and keep with the hands, arms or other means, grasp; clutch

Jar—A container made of glass, stone, or earthenware cylindrical with a large opening and no sprout; some have handles

Kind—Essential character, sort, variety, class

Knife—A cutting or stabbing instrument with a sharp blade, single edged or double edged, set in a handle

Large—Generous, big, great, taking up much space

Layers—A single thickness, coat, fold or stratum

Less—To diminish, meager; not so much

Loam—A rich soil composed of clay, sand, and some organic matter.

Longest—Measuring much from end to end in space or from beginning to end in time; not short or brief

Maker—A person of thing that makes (in various sense)

Masking—A covering for the face or a part of the face. To conceal or cover or disguise. To hide one's true motives character

Material—Of matter; of substance; relating to, or consisting of what occupies space; what a thing is or may be made of elements; parts of constituents

Measure—The extent, dimensions, capacity

Medium—Something intermediate, a middle state of degree; mean

Most—Greatest in amount; quantity, or degree; used as the superlative of much

Mouth—The opening through which an animal takes in food; chew

Much—to a great degree or extent; just alike, just about.

Mud—Wet, soft, sticky earth

Move—To change the place or position of, push, carry, or pull from one place or position to another

Particles—An extremely small piece; tiny fragment; the slightest trace speck

Piece—A part of fragment broken from the whole

Plants—A living organism that, unlike an animal has the ability to synthesize food from carbon dioxide possesses cellulose cell walls and lacks centrosomes specialized sense organs and digestive nervous and circulatory systems

Plastic—Molding or shaping matte; formative

Pour—To cause to flow in a continuous stream

Pushed—To exert pressure or force against, esp. so as to move.

Quarter—Any of the four equal parts of something, fourth

Quickly—Rapid; swift; done with promptness; lasting only a moment

Rim—An edge; border, or margin

Rubber—A thing that rubs as in polishing scraping massaging

Sand—Loose, gritty particles of worn of disintergrated rock varying in size, deposited along the shores of bodies of water.

Scissors—A cutting instrument, smaller than shears with two opposing blades each having a looped handle which or pivoted together in the middle so that they work against each other as the instrument is closed on the material to be cut

Smaller—Little in size, when compared with others of the same kind; not large or big limited in size

Soil—The surface layer of earth, supporting plant life

Space—Distance extending in all directions

Stays—To continue in the place or condition specified; to live, dwell, keep

Stocking—A close fitting covering usually knitted for the foot and most of the leg

Tape—A strong narrow, woven strips of cotton, lined, binds seems in garments, tie, bundles

Third—Proceeded by two others in series

Three—The cardinal number between two and four

Through—In one side and out the other side of; from end to end

Time—Indefinite, unlimited duration in which things are considered as happening in the past, present, or future; every moment ever been or will be

Two—The cardinal number between one and three

Type—A thing or event that represents or symbolizes another

Watch—Close observation for a time; in order to see or find out something

Water—The colorless, transparent liquid occurring on earth as rivers, lakes, oceans and falling from the clouds as rain.

Width—The fact, quality or condition of being wide; wideness

Without—Outside of a building or place not with

ASSESSMENTS

Preassessments—Understanding vocabulary words used in the lesson.

Postassessment—Completely understanding the first-hand experiments and verbal discussions.

Vocabulary options: Use, charts visual materials, songs, poems, films and appropriate level movies.

Parent involvement during lessons

Suggested Resources
to visit your
classrooms

Dentists
Optometrists
Nurses (RN)
Active Fitness Experts
Forecasters (T.V. or Radio)
A Baker (a cook)
A person with Astronautic Knowledge

CPSIA information can be obtained at www.ICGtesting.com
Printed in the USA
LVOW110931161012

303058LV00003B/73/P